Contents

	Page
What is the time?	4
What is 'time'?	6
Sundials and shadow clocks	8
Stars and star-clocks	10
The water clock	12
The sand clock	14
Fire clocks: candles and lamps	16
The first mechanical clocks	18
Weights, springs and pendulums	20
A great clock-maker	22
Navigation at sea	24
John Harrison and the marine chronometer	26
The first watches	28
The long-case clock and the wall clock	30
More than time	32
Quartz crystal and atomic clocks	34
Clock time and sundial time	36
Time-zones and the International Date Line	38
Earth, sun and seasons	40
The sun calendar and Ancient Egypt	42
The moon calendar	44
The calendar of Julius Caesar	46
The calendar of Pope Gregory	48
Our world and the Great Year	50

TIME, CALENDARS and CLOCKS

by ROY WORVILL, M.Sc.

with illustrations by
B. H. ROBINSON

Ladybird Books Ltd   Loughborough

What is the time?

Perhaps you remember playing a game called 'What's the time, Mr. Wolf?'. You may also know the old song which says 'If you want to know the time, ask a policeman'. There is probably no question in any language which is asked more frequently and none which is more easily answered. In the streets of our towns and cities you are seldom far from a clock. In remote country places, the radio and television bring very accurate time signals, which are increasingly necessary in an age which regulates so much of our lives by the hour and even by the minute.

We now take accurate time-keeping so much for granted that it is hard to imagine a world without clocks and watches. Yet the mechanical clock is a comparatively recent invention in the history of mankind. Our finest modern clocks, which are so accurate that they will not gain or lose as much as one second in hundreds of years, are the result of much experiment and research by scientists and inventors.

The first serious attempt to measure the passing of time, of which we have any certain knowledge, took place in Egypt about 3,000 years ago. It was in Egypt, too, at about the same period that men began to discover how to measure and survey their land. In this book you will read of the first simple measures of time and how they gradually developed into the modern clock. But first let us ask another question.

0 7214 0336 0

What is 'time'?

Answering our first question—what is the time?—usually presents little difficulty. By leaving out one short word—'the'—we now ask a very different question—'what is time?'. There is nothing in the world which is measured so often, yet remains such a complete mystery, as time. Most of the things we need to measure can be seen. Others, like an electric current for example, cannot be seen but at least are well understood.

A good clock or watch will show time passing at a steady, uniform rate. However, we often get the impression of time going more quickly at some periods than at others. If we are busily occupied with something interesting, the time seems to pass more quickly than it does if we are waiting in the rain for a bus. People often say that time passes more quickly as they grow older. The poet William Wordsworth told us that his days as a child seemed twenty times longer than the days when he was writing his poems.

Stop for a few moments and look at the hand of a clock or watch as it passes over a one minute space. It may seem quite a long time as you watch the hand but, long or short, it is a minute that will never return. Previously it was part of the future. As you turned your eyes from the dial it became part of history, joining the long ages which make up the four thousand million years or more which, some scientists tell us, have passed since the universe of suns and stars began.

'Time' can mean so many things

Sundials and shadow clocks

The earth's daily rotation on its axis seems to make the sun, moon, stars and planets move across the sky. These movements were observed for thousands of years before a true explanation of them was understood. The three main parts of the day must have been recognised very early in history. The time from sunrise to noon gives the morning, or forenoon interval, followed by the downward movement of the sun during the afternoon and then the night-long time of darkness.

The changing length and direction of shadows from trees, rocks and hills must have suggested the possibility of pushing a stick into the ground and making divisions on the ground, perhaps with stones, enabling the progress of its shadow to be followed more easily. This was the first kind of shadow clock, or sundial.

There must have been many such shadow clocks, but the earliest known sundial, which can still be seen in a Berlin museum, is believed to have been made in Egypt about 3,000 years ago. This form of dial is shown in the picture. Notice the unequal divisions along the bar. These compensate for the uneven speed of the shadow, which moves more quickly near sunrise and sunset than it does during the middle of the day. There are also some differences in the speed of the shadow through the course of the year. You will read more about this in the section about Greenwich Mean Time.

Later sundials became ornamental as their use declined. You may see them still in gardens, engraved with such words as 'Seize the present moment, the evening hour is nigh', or 'I tell only the sunny hours'.

A Primitive Shadow Clock

Egyptian Sundial

Stars and star-clocks

Our early ancestors must have been puzzled by the changing shape of the moon, and by the movements of the planets. However, they would have noticed that in the northern part of the sky some groups of stars (called constellations) can be found on any clear night of the year. You have probably seen some of them— one is the W-shaped constellation called *Cassiopeia* (also called *The Lady in the Chair*) and another is *The Little Bear*. These circumpolar constellations, as they are called, go round the north pole of the sky (marked approximately by the Pole star) once every day.

The brightest and largest of these circumpolar constellations is *The Plough*, which is sometimes called *The Big Dipper*. Because these stars travel round the Pole star like the hand of a clock moving round a dial, they can be used as time-keepers.

A star-clock, or *nocturnal* as it is called, can easily be made to tell the time by the position of the Plough stars. The picture opposite shows how the nocturnal worked. It was marked with the dates from January to December, and with the hours from one to twenty-four. The handle (A) was set to the date. With the Pole star sighted through the central hole, the finger (B) was turned until it was in line with the two stars named *The Pointers*. It then showed the time on the dial.

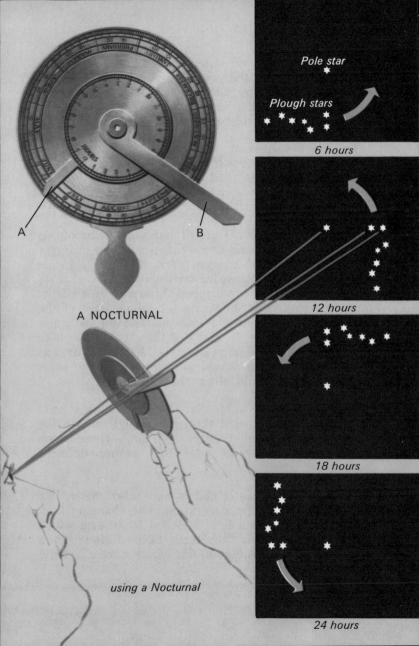

A NOCTURNAL

using a Nocturnal

A

B

Pole star

Plough stars

6 hours

12 hours

18 hours

24 hours

The water clock

The steady flow of water in a stream or river is often compared to the passing of time. The constant ebb and flow of the tides, too, has frequently been associated with time, as we are reminded by the saying—'Time and tide wait for no man'.

It is not surprising, therefore, that water slowly dripping from a bowl, or some other form of container, has been used to measure time. Such a 'clock' is called a *clepsydra*, from a Greek word meaning 'a water thief'.

The first water clocks are probably about as old as the shadow clocks, and one which was found in Egypt in 1904 is believed to date from 1400 BC. In its simplest form the clepsydra consisted of a bowl from which the water slowly dripped through a small hole, and the hours were shown by the falling level of the water measured against a scale marked on the inner surface of the bowl. In many of these bowls the hole was drilled through a pearl embedded in it. It was supposed that water would not wear away the pearl as quickly as it would other materials.

Another type of water clock used a floating bowl into which water passed through a small hole in the base, gradually causing the bowl to sink. These bowls were made in various sizes to measure different intervals of time.

More elaborate water clocks were also made, like the one shown in the illustration. The changing level of the water moves a float attached to an arm which has a serrated edge. The teeth fit into those on a wheel, and the turning of the wheel moves a hand round the dial.

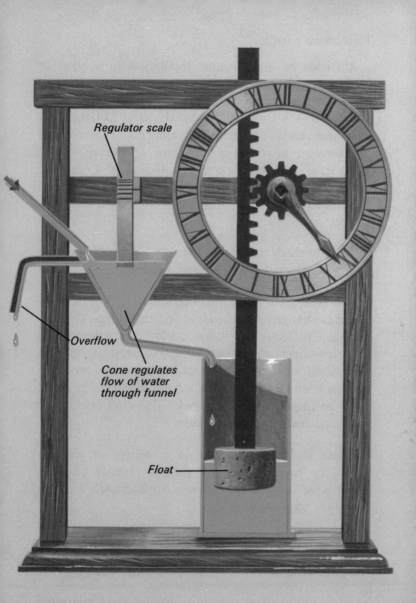

Regulator scale

Overflow

Cone regulates
flow of water
through funnel

Float

A CLEPSYDRA OR WATER CLOCK

The sand clock

A trickle of sand from a small hole in a bowl or bucket can obviously perform much the same purpose in measuring time as a steady drip of water. Consequently, it is not surprising that the sand or hour-glass has been used for centuries and even survives in our modern kitchens in the form of the egg-timer. There is a very old one in the House of Commons at Westminster which measured the interval of two minutes for the ringing of the bells calling the members to vote.

Sand is easily obtained in most places and, unlike water, it does not freeze in cold weather.

The sand-glass came into use about 1,200 years ago and has changed very little during that time. To keep the sand perfectly dry it was enclosed in a watertight glass container, which narrowed to a very fine tube in the middle section. The container was either mounted in a rack which could be turned upside-down, or could itself be turned within the rack. The sand could flow back and forth again and again.

These glasses were made in a variety of sizes to allow the measurement of various periods of time. Some were used at sea by early voyagers when calculating the ship's speed.

Some old churches still possess the hour-glasses which once indicated the slowly-passing minutes of the hour-long sermons which were usual years ago.

14   **A sand clock**

Fire clocks: candles and lamps

The steady burning of the flame of a candle or lamp suggested another way of measuring the passage of time. Fire clocks were used by the Chinese many centuries ago, and were described in the records of travellers to the East as recently as the mid-1800s.

Some fire clocks were even used as alarm clocks. They were described as 'sweet-smelling sticks', made by mixing clay with several different kinds of fragrant wood in the form of sawdust, to which musk and gold dust were also added. These would burn for several days. At various intervals down the length of the taper, small weights were suspended from a fine thread. The taper stood in a metal tray or bowl made of copper or brass. As the taper burned down, the thread was severed by the flame. The weights dropped into the bowl and the noise was supposed to awaken the sleeper.

Various forms of oil lamp were also used. The oil was stored in a transparent container, rather like the glass bowls you may still see in some antique oil lamps. A wick was lighted and as the oil level fell, the passing hours were shown by the divisions on the side of the container, divisions rather like those you see on medicine bottles and kitchen measures.

The candle clock is said to have been first used by King Alfred the Great a thousand years ago. Some candle clocks merely had lines marked at intervals down the length of the candle to indicate how much had been burned. Others had alternating layers of different coloured wax to serve the same purpose. All fire clocks had one great disadvantage; any draught could upset the rate of burning.

A candle clock

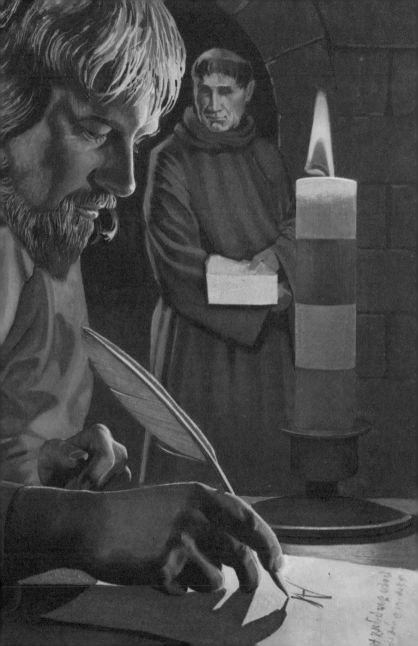

The first mechanical clocks

The inventor of the first mechanical clock is unknown. However, various names have been suggested, even that of Archimedes who lived in Greece about 250 BC.

In 1288, a clock was built at Westminster, London and was known as Great Tom. It is said to have been paid for by the money from a fine imposed upon a judge who was convicted of dishonesty in his duties.

About 1360 a famous clock, which still works, was made for the King of France, Charles V. It was placed in a tower of the King's palace and its single hand was driven by a 500 lb. weight. Like most early clocks it was not a good time-keeper and was often wrong by as much as two hours a day.

Although we always think of a clock telling the time by one or two hands moving round a dial, it is probable that most of the first clocks had neither hands nor dial. The word 'clock' really means a bell. An iron clock in Salisbury Cathedral is one of the oldest in Britain. It was made in 1386 and has no dial or hands but just strikes the hours from 1 to 12 on a bell. Another early clock, at Wells Cathedral, shows the phases of the moon and, every hour, figures of knights on horseback charge towards each other. The original mechanism is now in the Science Museum. Inside the cathedral another figure strikes the time on a bell.

The first clocks for use in the home began to appear in the late 1300s or early 1400s. They were made of iron, open on three sides and with only one hand.

The mechanism of a bell clock

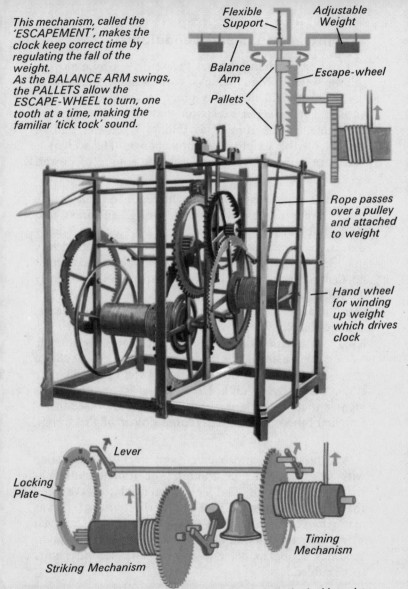

This mechanism, called the 'ESCAPEMENT', makes the clock keep correct time by regulating the fall of the weight.
As the BALANCE ARM swings, the PALLETS allow the ESCAPE-WHEEL to turn, one tooth at a time, making the familiar 'tick tock' sound.

Flexible Support

Adjustable Weight

Balance Arm

Escape-wheel

Pallets

Rope passes over a pulley and attached to weight

Hand wheel for winding up weight which drives clock

Lever

Locking Plate

Timing Mechanism

Striking Mechanism

A pin on a timing wheel lifts a lever from a notch in the locking plate, releasing the mechanism to strike the bell until the lever falls into the next notch.

Weights, springs and pendulums

The first mechanical clocks were driven by a slowly-falling weight. Many clocks with weights are still in use. The weight has one great advantage over the spring. The power it exerts on the mechanism remains the same all the time it is falling, since the pull of gravity on the weight does not change. The weight is therefore a more steady and reliable source of power.

In the later years of the fifteenth century some clocks were made with coiled springs of brass and steel, but these springs did not provide the steady power of a falling weight. As the spring slowly uncoiled, its power became weaker. The clock might go fast when it was fully wound and then too slowly as the spring unwound. This difficulty was at last overcome by the use of a small device called a *fusee*, a cone-shaped wheel with a spiral groove carrying a length of catgut or light chain. The wheel driving the clock mechanism was at the large end. The gut, or chain, unwound first from the small end of the fusee when the clock was fully wound. Here the effort required was greater than at the larger end. The tapering fusee therefore smoothed out the weakening power of the spring.

Another great improvement in clock-making came with the use of the pendulum. The Italian mathematician and scientist, Galileo, is believed to have been the first to suggest it, but the earliest use of it was made in Holland by Huygens about 1660. The even swing of the pendulum enabled clocks of great accuracy to be made, and minute and second hands to be added.

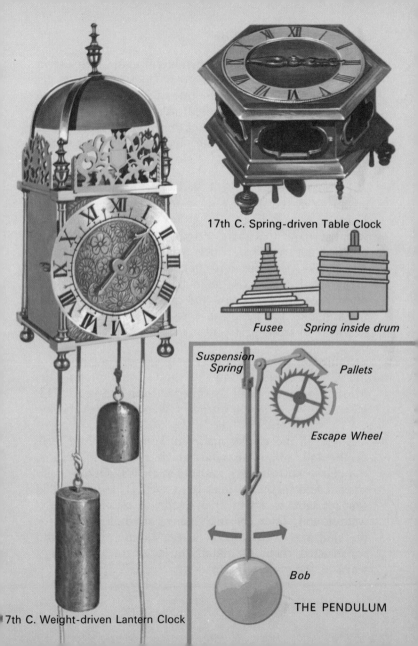

17th C. Spring-driven Table Clock

Fusee Spring inside drum

Suspension Spring

Pallets

Escape Wheel

Bob

THE PENDULUM

7th C. Weight-driven Lantern Clock

A great clock-maker

In 1664, soon after the pendulum came into use, a young man who became a great clock-maker was an apprentice in London. His name was Thomas Tompion and he was the son of a Bedfordshire blacksmith. He may have worked as a blacksmith himself before he ventured into clock-making, but of this we are not completely sure.

Tompion's great skill led to many important advances in the making of watches as well as clocks. Using a new kind of spring, invented by an English scientist named Robert Hooke, Tompion made one of the first watches which would keep good time. His clocks, watches and barometers were found in many royal palaces. Some of his clocks are still in use after three hundred years and must be counted among the valuable and beautiful treasures which have come down to us from past centuries.

Skilled clock-makers of his time were members of the Clockmakers' Company, and Tompion was its Master for nine years. At his death, in the year 1713, he was honoured by a burial in Westminster Abbey.

Some of the clocks made in Tompion's time were of the tall, long-case kind which afterwards became popularly known as grandfather clocks. Others were smaller and made to stand on a shelf. These are called bracket clocks. Their finely-made cases of ebony or walnut and, later, of mahogany, are noteworthy for the skill and craftmanship of the cabinet makers who constructed them to match the accurate and elegant work of the great clock-makers.

Thomas Tompion
1639-1713

Bracket Clock by Tompion

Navigation at sea

The early explorers did not venture very far from a coast. Even after the magnetic compass came into use, sailors could only give very rough estimates of the position of their ship. When Columbus sighted land at the end of his Atlantic voyage in 1492, he thought he was close to India.

It was becoming clear that a new and more accurate way of finding their position was needed by explorers and sailors, otherwise a sea voyage would continue to be a very dangerous adventure. Various suggestions were made to encourage scientists and inventors. Spain was a leading sea-power and, in 1598, King Philip III offered a rich reward for an improved method of navigation at sea. In Holland, too, a similar prize was offered.

A sailor can find his latitude, the distance north or south of the equator, by measuring the height of the sun at noon, or of the Pole Star on a clear night. Quite a simple instrument will do this. The great difficulty was to find the other measurement the sailor needs— his longitude, the distance east or west of the Greenwich meridian which means, roughly, how far east or west he is from London.

It was to help solve this problem that the Royal Greenwich Observatory was founded in 1675 by King Charles II. The observatory was moved a few years ago to the clearer air of Herstmonceux in Sussex and it is now concerned with many other departments of astronomy.

Not for another eighty years, however, was the most important new step forward made. This was the invention of a really accurate timekeeper for use in the hard conditions at sea. No pendulum clock would work on a rolling ship.

A captain uses a quadrant to calculate his latitude

John Harrison and the marine chronometer

It is very important that a clock or watch for use at sea should be as accurate as possible. Anything more than a very small error could result in an estimate many miles different from the ship's true position.

Among those who worked on the problem of obtaining complete accuracy was a watch-repairer named John Harrison, who lived in Yorkshire. He first brought his ideas to London in 1735, but it was not until many years later that one of his watches was taken on a voyage, lasting five months, to the West Indies and back. During the voyage it was found that the watch worked well and, at the end, its total error was less than two minutes. However, it was several more years, in 1764, before Harrison collected the promised reward of £20,000. Sad to say, he did not live long to enjoy the fruits of his labours. He died three years later. During the past two hundred years, generations of seafarers have had good reason to be grateful for his achievement, which removed some, at least, of the hazards of the sea.

Harrison's chronometer was made in the shape of an ordinary pocket watch, though larger, with a diameter of a little over five inches. Rubies and diamonds were used to reduce, as much as possible, the wear caused by the moving wheels.

A famous French watchmaker named Pierre Le Roy, who lived at the same time as Harrison, made some additional improvements, one of which was to mount the chronometer in a protective box with gimbals. Gimbals are short axles which enable the chronometer to swing freely, rather like a sailor in a hammock, so avoiding being tilted as the ship rolls.

John Harrison and his
prize-winning chronometer

The Royal Observatory, Greenwich, in 1675

The first watches

Telling the time has always been a matter of importance to travellers. Small sun-dials were sometimes carried for this purpose. Under cloudy skies and during the hours of darkness, however, the sundial was useless, and it was difficult to carry a clock on a journey. The need for a small, portable time-keeper led to the invention of the first watches, which were made about two hundred years before Harrison constructed his famous, prize-winning chronometer for use at sea.

The very first watch is believed to have been made by a German locksmith named Peter Henlein, about the year 1510. Early examples of the watch-maker's craft were usually made in the shape of a sphere and were too large to put in any normal pocket, even if there had been pockets in those days. When watches were made smaller it became the fashion to wear them round the neck, and the watch-case often contained some sweet-smelling perfume as well as the works.

Watch-making began in Britain towards the end of the sixteenth century and Queen Elizabeth I was a collector of fine watches. One of them was small enough to form part of a bracelet and this must have been one of the earliest wrist-watches. From this time onwards, watch-making in Britain began to flourish and some craftsmen became famous for their work. One of them, Edward East, was the official watch-maker to King Charles I.

Although the first watches were not very good time-keepers, they became popular as a form of jewellery and were worn by both men and women. The cases were made of many different materials, crystal and ivory as well as gold and silver. Their shapes show even more variety, such as shells, flowers, fruit and even skulls, and a large number of commoner geometrical forms.

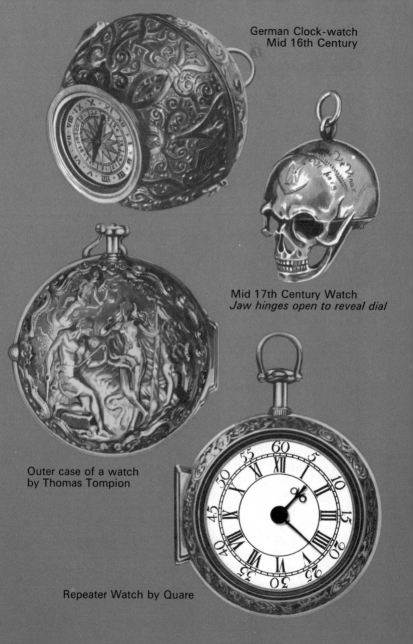

German Clock-watch
Mid 16th Century

Mid 17th Century Watch
Jaw hinges open to reveal dial

Outer case of a watch
by Thomas Tompion

Repeater Watch by Quare

The long-case clock and the wall clock

The long-case clock is now more often called the grandfather clock, and it is a form of clock which has been made throughout the last three hundred years in a great variety of designs. Similar clocks of smaller size, below about five feet in height, are sometimes called grandmother clocks.

Clocks which were driven by falling weights obviously needed room for the weights to drop and so were not suited to standing on a piece of furniture or mantel-shelf. They were often made in the form of the lantern-clock which stood on a bracket fixed to a wall. When it was thought an improvement to enclose the weights and chains inside a case, the grandfather clock was the result.

The first ones usually had square, brass dials but, just as fashions in dress and furniture changed, so did styles in clocks. Later dials became larger and were arched at the top. The chapter ring, as the circle containing the figures was called, was often silvered and skilfully engraved. A small hole in the dial sometimes showed the date on a revolving wheel. The corners of the dial were fitted with decorative patterns called spandrels and most dials carried the name of the clock-maker. Sometimes the owner's name was also engraved on the brass dial in elegant, scrolled lettering. Later dials, after about 1800, were made of iron and decorated with paint and enamels.

The case became an important part of the long-case clock and many different woods were used, such as intricate, inlaid walnut or marquetry, oak decorated in gold Chinese lacquer, and rich mahogany or fruitwood.

The earliest type of
long-case clock about 1660

Late 18th century long-case
clock with moon-phase dial

More than time

Although the most important feature of a watch or clock is that it should keep accurate time, many time-pieces were, and still are, very beautiful examples of craftsmanship. Makers tried hard to compete with their fellow-members of the Clock-makers' Company in producing clocks with some special feature. Many had a date-indicator, although this usually had to be adjusted by hand for months of less than thirty-one days.

The phases of the moon were frequently included in the arch of the clock dial. Some clocks made near seaports had dials for indicating the hours of high and low tide at those places.

There were clocks, and even some fine watches, which were fitted with musical chimes operated at intervals by the pins on the surface of a revolving drum or cylinder. As the drum turned, the pins set hammers striking a series of bells.

It would be impossible to describe all the immense variety of features which have been incorporated into clocks. Examples of these can be found in many museums and in antique shops. The swing of the pendulum has frequently been used to show moving eyes on the face of a human or animal figure. Sometimes you may see a clock which appears to have a stream of water gushing from a lion's head mask on the front of the case, but, when you look closely, you will find it is cleverly produced by a revolving glass rod, its surface fluted or twisted rather like a stick of barley-sugar. Most people want a clock to tell the time but such additions, like that of the cuckoo's call, add to the attraction of a clock.

An early alarm clock.
The clock opens the lid of
the tinder-box and sets
off the flintlock, which
ignites the tinder.
The lighted candle then
swings up.

A Swiss watch of 1800
with painted dial and
revolving windmill

The moon-phase
and tidal dial of a
grandfather clock

Quartz crystal and atomic clocks

Throughout the history of timekeeping we find that inventors, scientists and clock-makers have always been looking for new ideas and improvements which would produce greater accuracy. It has taken about 3,000 years to reach the stage at which we now have an answer to the question—'What's the time?'—which is far more accurate than we would ever need for normal everyday life.

One of the new timekeeping methods is provided by the quartz crystal clock. A clock of this kind is quite unlike the normal clock in appearance and is a very complicated piece of mechanism. It is based on the fact that a tiny crystal of quartz can be made to vibrate, by an electric current, at the rate of 100,000 times every second. In 1942 one was installed in the Royal Observatory, Greenwich, a very appropriate place because astronomers are very much concerned with accurate time-keeping. It was used to give the time-signal of six 'pips' broadcast by the B.B.C. in their radio programmes.

The atomic clock is another modern invention, so accurate that it will not gain or lose one second over hundreds of years. This works by tiny, vibrating particles called molecules. The ammonia molecule is one material used and the vibration takes place at a rate of many millions of times per second without variation. It controls a clock to a degree of accuracy that would certainly astonish the great clock-makers of three centuries ago, although it lacks the beautiful appearance and the pleasing charm of the familiar 'grandfather', quietly ticking away the seconds as it does in the corner of many homes today.

Temperature control circuit   Amplifier

Quartz Crystal

The quartz crystal and electrical connections which are in the concrete pier.

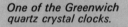

One of the Greenwich quartz crystal clocks.

A domestic quartz crystal clock with no moving parts. Illuminated bars show the time.

RIGHT: An atomic clock at the National Physical Laboratory.

Clock time and sundial time

Shadow clocks and sundials have an important disadvantage as time-keepers, quite apart from being useless at night and in cloudy weather. They depend upon the *apparent* movement of the sun. The shadow moves over the dial as the sun *appears* to travel from east to west across the sky.

As you know, what really happens is that the earth is turning on its axis. We are also moving round the sun every year along a path which is not quite circular. The earth's orbit round the sun, like those of all the planets, is an ellipse. We are about 3,000,000 miles nearer to the sun in January than we are in July.

Strange to say, this does not have any great effect upon our climate, but it does cause the sun's gravitational pull to vary in strength. This, in turn, affects the earth's speed and, together with the tilt of the earth's axis, makes the sun's apparent movement across the sky uneven through the year.

To overcome this difficulty, astronomers invented an imaginary body called the Mean Sun which is assumed to move at a steady speed, like a reliable clock. The sundial, which follows the motion of the real sun, is sometimes ahead of the clock showing Greenwich Mean Time and sometimes behind it. The diagram on the opposite page shows how these two time-keepers disagree with one another through the year. You will see that they are in step on only four days out of three hundred and sixty-five, where the red line crosses the thick blue one.

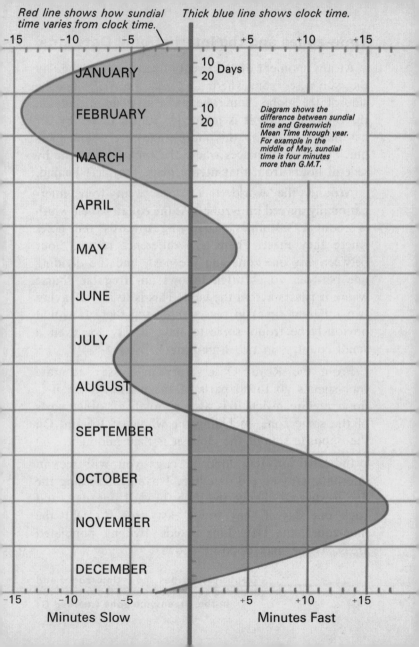

Time-zones and the International Date Line

At any moment of the twenty-four hours of the day the sun rises somewhere and sets on the opposite side of the globe. Somewhere else it is noon and, on the opposite side, it is midnight. Rapid travel by air has made us realize this more than ever. Travellers quickly arrive at places where the time is different by several hours from that at the place they left behind.

Around the world there are twenty-four internationally agreed time-zones. At the equator their width is about 1,000 miles, narrowing towards the poles where they meet. There is a difference of one hour between any one zone and the next, and the dividing line between zones often follows an irregular course where it passes across the land. This is to avoid having two different times in places close together. It would obviously be troublesome to have a city, or even a small country, in two time-zones!

From the Royal Observatory in Sussex accurate time-signals go to all parts of the world. When it is noon at Greenwich it is also noon in all other parts of the same zone, including the whole of Britain. On the opposite side of the globe it is then midnight.

Indicated on the opposite page you will see an internationally agreed date line. Travellers crossing the line westwards change the date forward one day, and back one day if they travel eastwards. As with the time-zones, the Date Line avoids dividing populated areas, as the map opposite shows.

Opposite: Stripes show time-zones and hours added to or subtracted from the time in the Greenwich zone (marked G)

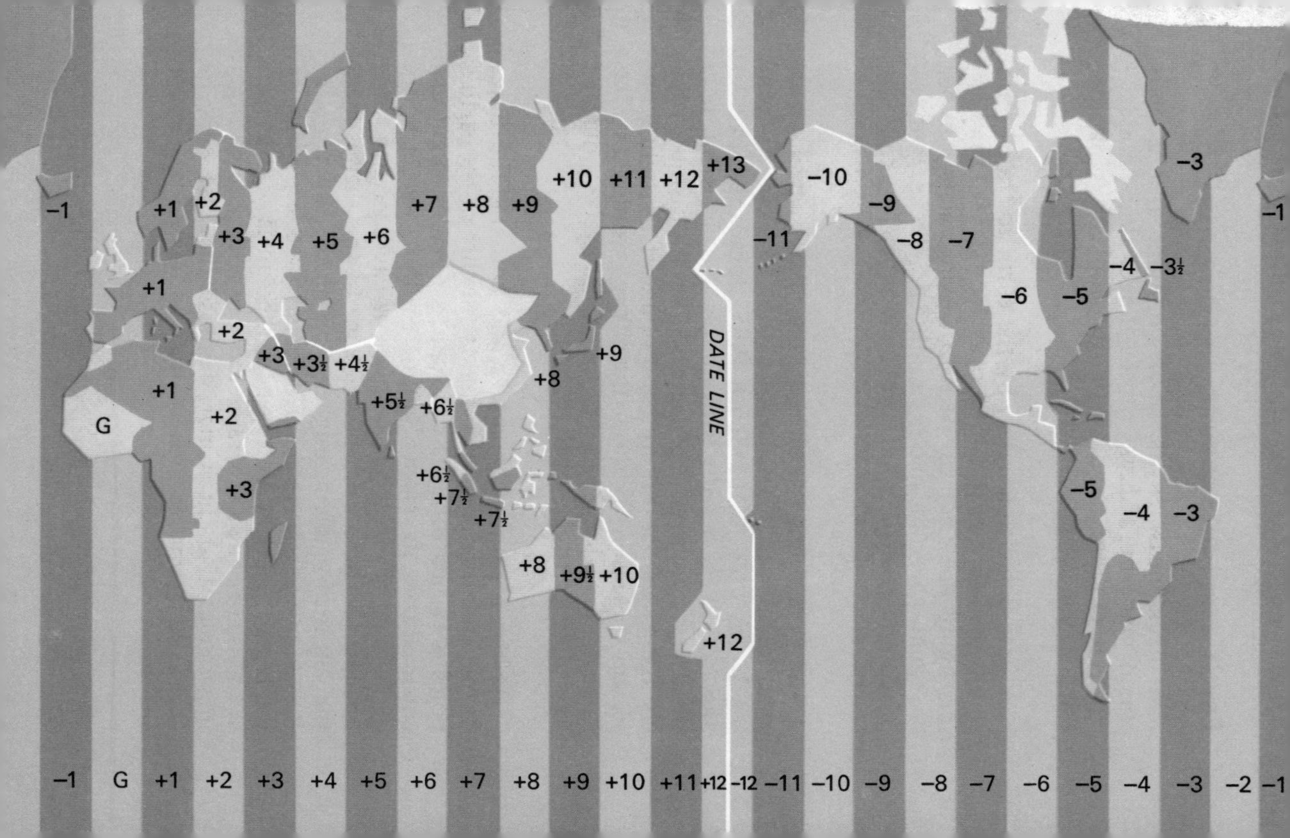
DATE LINE
–1
+1
+2
+3
+4
+5
+6
+7
+8
+9
+10
+11
+12
+13
–10
–9
–3
–1
–11
–8
–7
–6
–5
–4
–3½
+1
+2
+3
+3½
+4½
+9
+8
+1
+2
G
+5½
+6½
+3
+6½
+7½
+7½
+8
+9½
+10
–5
–4
–3
+12
–1
G
+1
+2
+3
+4
+5
+6
+7
+8
+9
+10
+11
+12
–12
–11
–10
–9
–8
–7
–6
–5
–4
–3
–2
–1

Earth, sun and seasons

A clock measures the hours, minutes and seconds which make up a day. For the longer time-periods—days, weeks and months—most people rely upon a calendar or diary.

A year is the time taken by the earth to travel once round the sun and is a little over 365¼ days. However, this figure does not divide into a convenient number of equal parts to make months or weeks, and so produced some difficult problems when making the calendar.

The earth spins round every day like a wheel on an axle, but the earth's axle (or axis as it is called) from the North Pole to the South Pole, does not make an angle of ninety degrees with the plane of its orbit. It is tilted at an angle of 23½ degrees. This tilt produces the changing weather patterns and hours of daylight from season to season. Without the tilt we would have the same season all the year round, with twelve hours of daylight and twelve of darkness.

At the beginning of spring and autumn, the times of the equinoxes, or 'equal nights', neither of the earth's poles is turned towards the sun, so day and night are equal all over the globe. Summer, with its longer hours of daylight and warmer weather, is caused by the axis turning one pole towards the sun. In that hemisphere the sun then reaches a higher point in the sky at noon. It is above the horizon for a longer time, especially in the region near the Pole, where the sun is visible even at midnight. The sun's rays, too, are felt more strongly in summer than in winter, because they are concentrated on a smaller area of the surface as the picture shows.

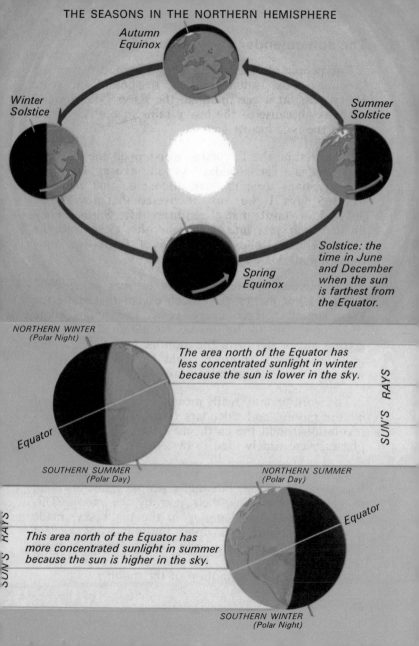

THE SEASONS IN THE NORTHERN HEMISPHERE

Autumn Equinox

Winter Solstice

Summer Solstice

Spring Equinox

Solstice: the time in June and December when the sun is farthest from the Equator.

NORTHERN WINTER
(Polar Night)

The area north of the Equator has less concentrated sunlight in winter because the sun is lower in the sky.

SUN'S RAYS

Equator

SOUTHERN SUMMER
(Polar Day)

NORTHERN SUMMER
(Polar Day)

SUN'S RAYS

This area north of the Equator has more concentrated sunlight in summer because the sun is higher in the sky.

Equator

SOUTHERN WINTER
(Polar Night)

The sun calendar and Ancient Egypt

The people of Ancient Egypt had a good reason for keeping a close watch upon the seasons of the year. Every year, at a certain time, the River Nile flooded its banks because of the heavy rains in central Africa where the Nile has its source.

At one time the Egyptians worshipped the sun and they used a solar calendar. As long ago as 4,000 BC the Egyptians seem to have discovered that the year has 365 days. It was not discovered that a year has $365\frac{1}{4}$ days until many centuries afterwards. They divided their year into twelve months; eleven months of thirty days followed by one of thirty-five, thus including all 365 days.

The missing quarter of a day (a year being $365\frac{1}{4}$ days) did not matter very much except that the error grew slightly bigger every year. Eventually, some correction had to be made, to avoid the seasons getting out of step with the months. Otherwise, as the centuries passed, summer could have arrived at the wrong time of the calendar year.

The word 'month' really means 'an interval measured by the moon', and calendars based upon the moon's revolution round the earth, as shown by its changing phases, were widely used in the Ancient World.

The solar calendar was very much better than one based on the moon, but many people were unwilling to give up measuring their year by the moon. This strange globe, ever-changing in the night sky, made a powerful impression upon the minds of ancient peoples. Many of us, even today, hold curious superstitions about it. The date of Easter is still worked out from the motion of the moon.

THE AUTUMN FLOODS IN EGYPT

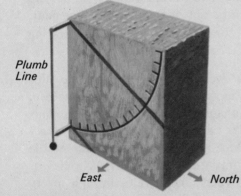

Plumb
Line

East   North

PTOLEMY'S PLINTH: A shadow
instrument, made of stone, for
measuring the angle of elevation
of the noon sun.

OBELISKS were probably used to determine
the time of noon i.e. When the shadow is at
its shortest.

The moon calendar

A calendar based on the movements of the moon had certain advantages to primitive peoples living in countries with clear skies. The time from one new moon or full moon to the next could be seen quite easily. It is 29½ days plus a few more minutes, and is called the synodical month. The task of watching the moon was entrusted to priests, and we still use the word 'synod' for a gathering of officials of the Church.

However, the synodical month of 29½ days was not an easy number to use on a calendar. It was more convenient to have months of 29 days and 30 days alternately. But six months of 29 days and six months of 30 days would give us a year of 354 days instead of 365. An error of this size would rapidly mount up and the seasons soon be out of step with the calendar, a difficult situation for people who lived by sowing seed and harvesting crops.

Various attempts were made to overcome this problem. One solution was to ignore the problem entirely, as the Mohammedan calendar does. This lags behind the solar calendar by eleven days every year. After thirty-three years it has lost one whole year and, during this time, the various religious festivals gradually work their way through every month of the year. If we followed the Mohammedan calendar in Europe, we should find Christmas, Easter and the seasons arriving at times different from those dates which are fixed by our present calendar. We could find that Christmas arrived in August!

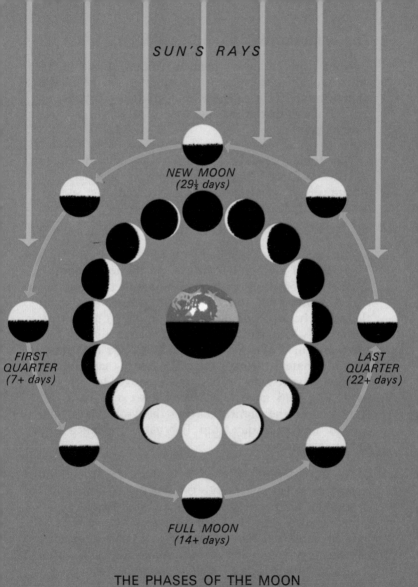

SUN'S RAYS

NEW MOON
(29½ days)

FIRST
QUARTER
(7+ days)

LAST
QUARTER
(22+ days)

FULL MOON
(14+ days)

THE PHASES OF THE MOON
*The outer ring shows the moon as seen from space and looking down
to the earth. The inner ring shows the various phases as we see them.*

The calendar of Julius Caesar

When the Romans invaded Britain about 2,000 years ago, their calendar was calculated on the phases of the moon. This calendar had gradually become so out of line with the seasons that it was two or three months behind!

The Emperor, Julius Caesar, was determined to correct it. Caesar had been to Egypt and seen the advantages of a calendar which used only the sun, so he sought help from a Greek astronomer who lived in the Egyptian city of Alexandria.

The astronomer's name was Sosigenes and his calendar had a year of 365 days. As the real length of a year is 365¼ days (within a few minutes), Sosigenes added another day to every fourth year. His calendar therefore became almost correct every fourth year. The year which had an extra day was called a *leap year*, and in it the months had thirty-one and thirty days alternately through the year. During each of the other three years one day had to be removed to leave 365 days. It would have been sensible to remove a day from one of the months having thirty-one days, but, instead, he took a day from February, leaving it with only twenty-nine.

The fifth month of their calendar (the seventh in ours) was called Julius (July), following the Emperor's death, and the next one was named Augustus (August) after his successor. It is said that Augustus wished to have his month as long as that of Julius and so another day was taken from February to make August equal in length to July, with thirty-one days each.

Caesar discusses the calendar with Sosigenes

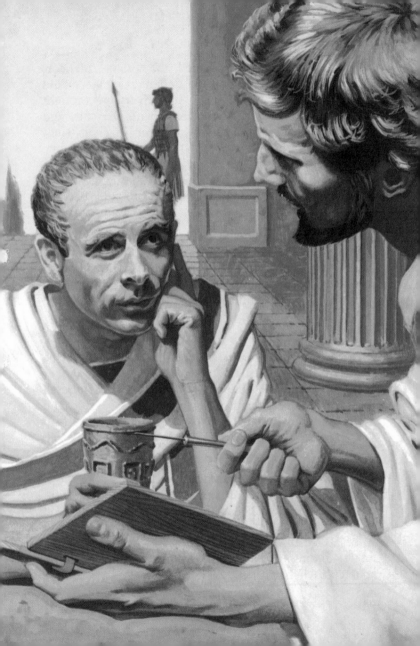

The calendar of Pope Gregory

Caesar's calendar was called the Julian calendar, and it seemed likely that the Julian calendar would remain unaltered for a long time. Everyone thought that it would keep in step exactly with the sun, and that the seasons would always occur in their right calendar months. However, nature still seemed to be awkward, for a year is actually eleven minutes less than 365¼ days. Over a few years this may not amount to very much, but a small error can eventually become a big one.

By 1500 the difference had become noticeable, for the gap between the calendar and the sun had widened to ten days, and the spring equinox was arriving on the calendar date of March 11th instead of March 21st. This was not very important to a farmer, but it was to the Church, which used the spring equinox, together with the moon's phases, to calculate the date of Easter.

In 1582, Pope Gregory ordered that a correction be made by advancing the date of October 5th to October 15th. To avoid the error creeping in again, he altered the leap year arrangement so that years like 1800 and 1900, centennial years, would not be counted as leap years unless the number could be divided exactly by 400.

Catholic countries, such as Spain and France, adopted the new calendar at once. In Britain, then mainly a Protestant country, the change was not made until September 2nd, 1752. By that time the old calendar was another day out and eleven days had to be added to the date, a change which aroused much anger among some people who thought it would shorten their lives!

An angry crowd protests against the new calendar

Our world and the Great Year

For every measurement we need a convenient unit, neither too large nor too small. From London to New York is too far to measure in inches or centimetres. Our lives are too long for seconds but too short for centuries. The year-long calendar serves us well for most purposes but, away from the earth, there are other kinds of 'years'.

Some planets are further away from the sun and therefore take longer to travel round it. Saturn's 'year' is nearly thirty times longer than ours. Neptune takes one hundred and sixty-five of our years to complete its orbit, and Pluto nearly two hundred and fifty.

Our earth is not only spinning on its axis every day and travelling round the sun every three hundred and sixty-five days; the axis itself is slowly changing direction. This was discovered by the Greeks many centuries ago. The northern end of the axis points to a position very close to that of the Pole star, but is gradually moving round a path which is nearly circular. In centuries to come, other stars will mark the north pole of the heavens and, similarly, the southern pole. The northern end of the axis completes this almost circular path in about 26,000 years, a period sometimes called the Great Year.

Our sun and its planets are only part of the vast star system called *The Galaxy*, or *Milky Way*. This, too, is revolving like a gigantic Catherine wheel of a hundred thousand million stars. We are moving round with it at a speed of about 150 miles every second, but a complete revolution takes over two hundred million years. It is all part of the unfathomable mystery of 'time'.

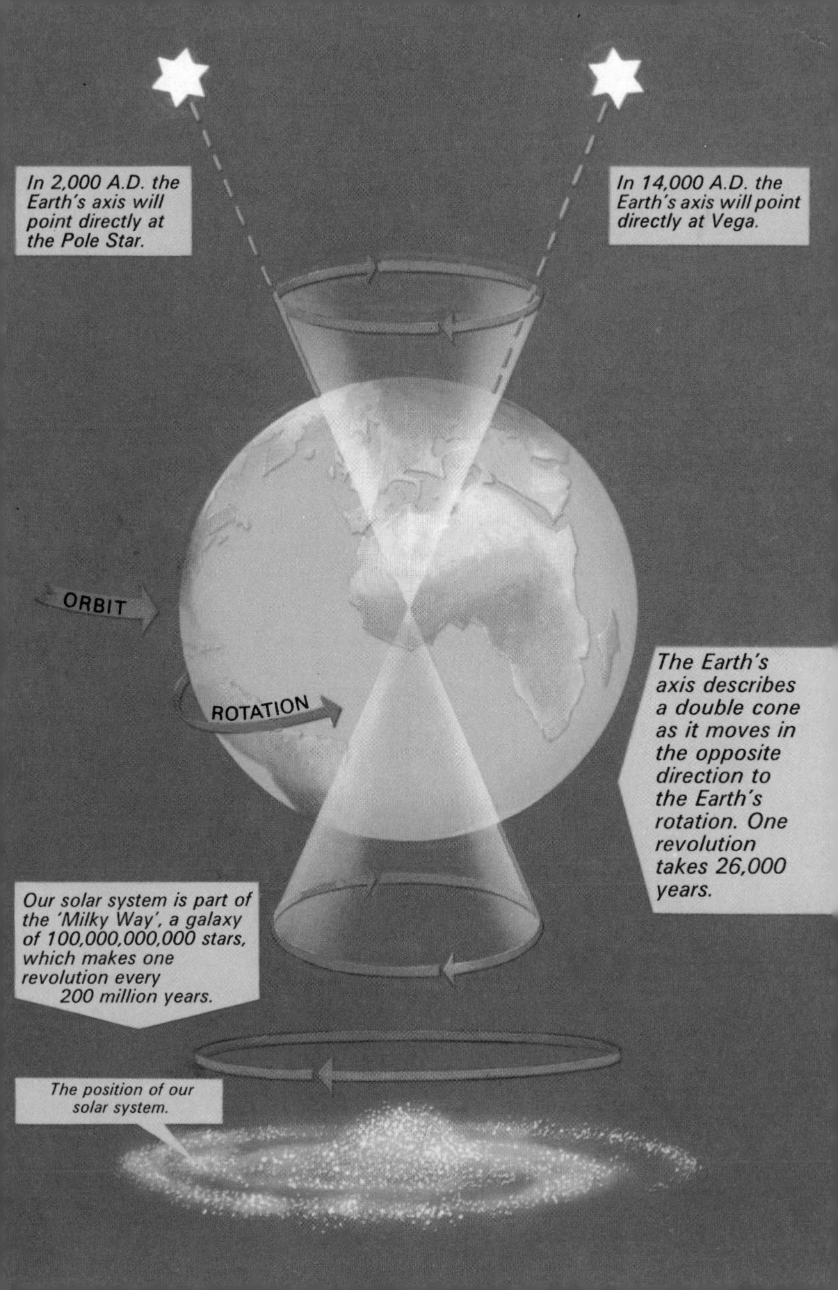

In 2,000 A.D. the Earth's axis will point directly at the Pole Star.

In 14,000 A.D. the Earth's axis will point directly at Vega.

ORBIT

ROTATION

The Earth's axis describes a double cone as it moves in the opposite direction to the Earth's rotation. One revolution takes 26,000 years.

Our solar system is part of the 'Milky Way', a galaxy of 100,000,000,000 stars, which makes one revolution every 200 million years.

The position of our solar system.